Alexander Graham Bell

Inventor of the Telephone

Carin T. Ford

Enslow Publishers, Inc.

40 Industrial Road   PO Box 38
Box 398   Aldershot
Berkeley Heights, NJ 07922   Hants GU12 6BP
USA   UK

http://www.enslow.com

Library of Congress Cataloging-in-Publication Data

Ford, Carin T.
  Alexander Graham Bell : inventor of the telephone / Carin T. Ford.
    p. cm. — (Famous inventors)
  Summary: A biography of the teacher and inventor best known for his work
  with the deaf and his invention of the telephone.
  Includes bibliographical references and index.
  ISBN 0-7660-1858-X (hardcover)
  1. Bell, Alexander Graham, 1847–1922—Juvenile literature. 2. Inventors—United States—
Biography—Juvenile literature. 3. Telephone—History. [1. Bell, Alexander Graham, 1847–1922.
  2. Inventors. 3. Telephone—History.] I. Title. II. Series.
  TK6143.B4 F67   2002
  621.385'092—dc21

                                                                    2002000391

Printed in the United States of America

10 9 8 7 6 5 4 3 2 1

To Our Readers: We have done our best to make sure all Internet Addresses in this book were active and appropriate when we went to press. However, the author and the publisher have no control over and assume no liability for the material available on those Internet sites or on other Web sites they may link to. Any comments or suggestions can be sent by e-mail to comments@enslow.com or to the address on the back cover.

Every effort has been made to locate all copyright holders of material used in this book. If any errors or omissions have occurred, corrections will be made in future editions of this book.

Illustration Credits: Gilbert H. Grosvenor Collection, Library of Congress, pp. 3, 4, 7, 8, 12, 20, 26, 27, 28; Library of Congress, pp. 11, 13, 15, 17, 21, 22; Library of Congress, illus. Howard Jones, pp. 8–9; Library of Congress, painted by William A. Rogers, pp. 24–25; Photo courtesy of Western Union Financial Services, Inc., p. 16.

Cover Credits: Gilbert H. Grosvenor Collection, Library of Congress

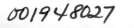

Table of Contents

Alexander Graham Bell was known as Aleck.

Chapter 1

Early Sounds

A lexander Graham Bell was always listening. When he was just a little boy, he ran into the middle of a wheat field one day and sat down. Aleck stayed that way for a long time . . . listening. He was trying to hear the wheat grow.

Aleck spent most of his life listening to all the sounds around him. His father and grandfather were both speech teachers. They helped people who could not speak clearly. Aleck learned everything he could about sound and speech. These studies would one day lead to his invention of the telephone.

Aleck was born on March 3, 1847, in Edinburgh, Scotland. He was the second of Alexander and Eliza Bell's three sons. When Aleck was eleven, he decided he wanted a middle name. He chose *Graham* because it had a strong sound to it. From then on, he used the name Alexander Graham Bell.

At first Aleck did not go to school. Instead, his mother taught him at home. He learned to read, spell, and do math. He was a shy boy but always very creative.

Aleck came up with his first invention one day when he was at his friend Ben's house. Ben's father owned a mill for grinding wheat into flour. He saw

Eliza and Alexander Bell with their sons, from left to right, Melville, Edward, and Aleck.

Ben and Aleck playing. "Go do something useful," he said. He told them to find a way to clean the husks off the small grains of wheat.

Aleck began to experiment. He put together a barrel and some brushes to strip the outer coats from the wheat. His machine worked!

> Aleck loved to make discoveries.

Aleck was sent to school when he was ten. He did not like it very much and was bored most of the time. He did well in reading but not in his other subjects.

Aleck was happier learning about the world by himself. He

collected plants and birds' eggs. He studied dogs, cats, rabbits, mice, guinea pigs, frogs, and toads. Aleck never killed an animal himself. But if

Aleck learned about nature by studying plants and birds' eggs.

he found a dead mouse or bird, he would cut it open to see its insides. He was always interested in discovering something new.

Chapter 2

How Do People Speak?

Aleck's mother was almost deaf, but she still loved playing the piano. She used a long ear-tube to hear the music. One end was at her ear; the other was attached to the piano.

Mrs. Bell gave her son piano lessons, and he became a very good musician. For a while, he dreamed of becoming a famous piano player. Sometimes Aleck could not sleep because he heard music in his head all through the night.

When Aleck was fifteen, he was sent to London, England, to stay with his grandfather. His parents thought that he could learn more there than in school. Grandfather Bell took good care of Aleck and made sure the boy paid careful attention to his studies.

Old Mr. Bell had a large library in his home filled with books on sound. Aleck read about how sound is sent and received. He learned many new things that year.

Aleck returned to Scotland when he was sixteen. One day his father challenged

Aleck's mother holds an ear-tube. Putting one end near her ear helped her to hear better.

him to build a machine that could talk. Aleck and his brother Melville went right to work. At the butcher, they got the voice box from the neck of a lamb. They studied it, then made one out of tin and rubber.

Next the boys shaped the head for their speaking machine. They used a rubbery material to form the tongue and mouth. When they blew into the mouth, it said, "Mama! Mama!" It sounded just like a baby's cry. Several neighbors came running outside to see what was wrong!

The project was fun for Aleck. But he also learned something very important: He found out how people are able to talk and make sounds.

Grandfather Bell was a kind man. He taught Aleck many things.

Growing up, Aleck loved music and reading.

Chapter 3

More Experiments

Sixteen-year-old Aleck took a job teaching music and speech at a school. He was younger than some of his students, but he was a very good teacher.

Aleck spent the next few years teaching at different schools while going to college in England and Scotland. He studied how people use their lips, tongue, and voice box to speak. He learned how ears are able to hear.

Aleck decided to experiment with his family dog, Trouve. He wanted to teach Trouve how to speak. First he trained Trouve to growl. Then Aleck stuck his hand into the dog's mouth. When he pressed different places in the dog's throat, Aleck could change the sound of the growl. Soon the dog was able to say, "Ow-ah-oo gamama." This sounded like, "How are you, grandmama?"

Aleck was a very good teacher.

Aleck's family thought this was wonderful. So did the dog. He even stood on his hind legs and tried to talk by himself!

In his free time, Aleck experimented with batteries, telegraph wires, and electricity. He was interested in the telegraph, which had been invented by

Before telephones, people used telegraph machines to send messages.

Samuel Morse in the 1830s. It used electric pulses to send messages over a wire. The messages sounded like clicks, and Morse wrote a code using patterns of clicks to stand for letters and numbers. For example, in Morse code, three short clicks is an s.

Aleck imagined that someday, electric pulses could be used to send the human voice—not just clicks or sounds—over the wires.

Mr. Bell encouraged his son to do more experiments. By this time, Aleck's father had become well known. He had drawn many pictures to show how the lips, tongue, and throat must move to make the sounds we use when we talk. He called his drawings Visible Speech.

Mr. Bell used Visible Speech to teach deaf people

how to speak. He traveled all over and talked about his work. Aleck gave some of the lectures, too.

Aleck's life changed greatly when his two brothers died. They both had tuberculosis, a disease of the lungs. Aleck's parents were very sad, and they worried

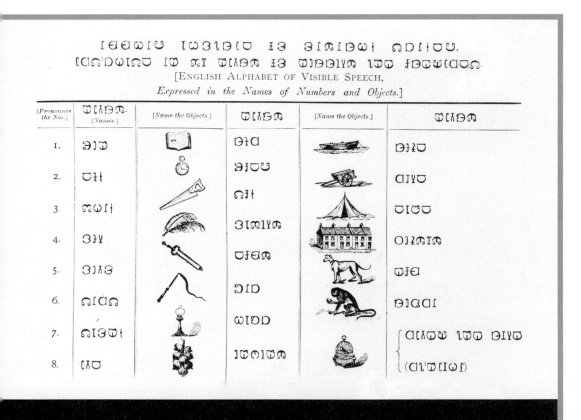

Aleck's father drew pictures of Visible Speech.

about Aleck, too. Often he did not feel well. He was tired and had headaches.

The Bells decided to move to Canada. They hoped the fresh air would make Aleck healthy again. The family sailed across the Atlantic Ocean in 1870. They settled in Brantford, Ontario.

Aleck played with tuning forks to learn about sounds.

Life in Canada seemed to agree with Aleck. He put on weight and had healthy color in his face. He also kept busy. He studied tuning forks. These are small metal tools that vibrate, or shake, and make a tone when they are struck. Different tuning forks make different sounds.

Aleck also spent long hours just sitting and doing what he had done since he was a little boy: He listened.

Chapter 4

Inventing the Telephone

Aleck traveled to Boston, Massachusetts, and became a teacher at the Boston School for the Deaf. He used his father's Visible Speech to teach children to talk.

One of Aleck's students was born deaf. She had never heard a sound. Aleck put the little girl's hand on his throat while he talked. He wanted her to feel the shaking—or vibrating—of his voice. This is what other people hear as sounds. Then she touched her

Mabel Hubbard became deaf when she was just a little girl.

own throat to copy him. This is how he taught her to speak.

Aleck's success at teaching deaf people to talk made him famous. In 1873, he became a professor at Boston University. He taught classes on how humans make sounds.

Aleck also did more experiments with electricity. He wanted to invent a "harmonic telegraph." It would be able to carry several messages over one wire at the same time. Soon, Aleck's idea went even further. Could electricity be used to carry the sound of the human voice?

During this time, Aleck was also giving speech lessons in his home. One student was five-year-old

George Sanders. He had been born deaf. Another was fifteen-year-old Mabel Hubbard. She had been deaf since the age of five, after being sick with scarlet fever.

Mabel's father was very interested in Aleck's experiments. He and George's father agreed to give Aleck money to do more research.

Aleck was now able to rent a workshop. He also hired Thomas Watson as his assistant. Watson was a skilled mechanic and electrician.

In 1875, Aleck Bell and Thomas Watson were working on the harmonic telegraph.

Thomas Watson helped Aleck with many experiments.

One day, a vibrating part became stuck, and Watson tried to fix the problem. He plucked at it with his finger. Bell was in another room, but he heard the sound that came over the wires.

The two men knew they were close to sending a human voice over the wires. They were very excited and worked even harder.

On March 10, 1876, Aleck spoke into his end of the equipment. Watson waited in another room with his ear pressed against the other end, which is called the receiver.

Bell's first telephone.

"Mr. Watson, come here, I want you," Aleck said. And Thomas Watson heard every word!

This invention was called the telephone.

Chapter 5

Scientist and Inventor

Bell's telephone became famous in 1876 when he showed the invention to a few of the world's top scientists. They were visiting Philadelphia for a world's fair.

A year later, Bell proved that his telephone could carry messages across many miles. He was in Boston, Massachusetts, and Watson was fifteen miles away in the city of Salem. With a wire strung between the cities, Bell and Watson talked to each other on the telephone.

Newspapers and magazines all over the United States, Canada, and Europe spread the news of Bell's amazing invention.

Bell gave more talks and demonstrations of the telephone. He earned some money from this. With his first profit from his invention, he bought Mabel Hubbard a small silver model of a telephone.

In 1877, Aleck and Mabel were married, and Aleck became a citizen of the United States. The Bells

In their lab, Aleck Bell and Thomas Watson were always busy with many projects.

now lived in Washington, D.C. They also had a summer home in Nova Scotia, Canada. Two daughters, Elsie and Marian, were born in the next few years.

The Bell Telephone Company was formed in July 1877. More and more people wanted this wonderful invention. At first, there were only about two hundred telephones in use. In time, there would be millions.

Bell became wealthy from inventing the telephone. He used some of his money to help other scientists and inventors. He also kept working on his own inventions throughout his life.

When President James Garfield was shot in 1881, Bell invented a metal detector to look for the bullet in his body. It did not help the president, who died. But it was later used in hospitals before X-ray machines were invented.

The Bell family, from left: Elsie, Mabel, Marian, and Aleck.

The Bells had a son in 1881. Their newborn baby had trouble breathing, and he died after a few hours. Bell was filled with sadness. He decided to invent a "vacuum jacket" that could force air in and out of a person's lungs. His work

**With his interest in flying machines,
Bell built many amazing kites.**

helped lead to today's iron lung, a machine that helps people breathe.

Bell was also interested in flying. Like many other inventors of his time, Bell wanted to create a flying machine. He experimented with several ideas, including kites in many different shapes. Bell even built kites that were big and sturdy enough to carry people. One day, some of Bell's discoveries would be used in the building of bridges. He also worked on hydrofoils—boats that skim across on top of the water.

With inventions and hard work, Aleck helped many people.

Alexander Graham Bell died on August 2, 1922. To honor him, all the telephones in the United States were silent for one minute when he was buried.

He was awarded many prizes and honors in his lifetime. Although he is best known as a scientist and inventor, Bell himself was most proud of teaching the deaf to speak.

Timeline

1847~Born in Edinburgh, Scotland.

1862~Lives for a year with his grandfather in London and reads about speech.

1870~Moves to Canada with his family.

1871~Moves to the United States to teach deaf students in Boston.

1874~Works on the harmonic telegraph.

1876~Invents the telephone.

1877~Marries Mabel Hubbard.

1891~Begins to experiment with flying machines.

1898~Becomes president of the National Geographic Society.

1907~Experiments with hydrofoils—boats that skim across the water.

1922~Dies on August 2 in Nova Scotia.

Words to Know

electricity—A form of energy. It is used to power lights and machines.

hydrofoil—A boat that skims across on top of the water.

Morse code—Patterns of sounds used for sending messages. Groups of long and short clicks—called dashes and dots—stand for letters and numbers.

telegraph—A device for sending messages from one place to another over wires.

tuning fork—A metal tool that always makes the same tone when it is hit. It is used to tune musical instruments.

voice box—The area in the throat where sounds are made.

world's fair—An event where people from all over the world share new ideas and inventions.

Learn More

Books

Fisher, Leonard Everett. *Alexander Graham Bell.* New York: Atheneum, 1999.

Gearhart, Sarah. *Telephone.* New York: Atheneum, 1999.

Matthews, Tom L. *Always Inventing: A Photobiography of Alexander Graham Bell.* Washington, D.C.: National Geographic Society, 1999.

Internet Addresses

The Alexander Graham Bell Family Collection
<http://bell.uccb.ns.ca/kidsindex.asp>

Alexander Graham Bell
<http://www.alexandergrahambell.org>

National Inventors Hall of Fame
<http://www.invent.org/hall_of_fame/11.html>

Index